MacBook Air 2020 User Manual
In 30 Minutes

A Guide to Tips, Tricks and Hidden Features of the 2020 MacBook Air for Beginners

KONRAD CHRISTOPHER

Copyright

Konrad Christopher
ISBN: 9798672390611
ChurchGate Publishing House
USA | UK | Canada
© Churchgate Publishing House 2020

All rights reserved. No part of this publication may be reproduced, stored in a retrieval system or transmitted in any form or by any means, electronic, mechanical, photocopying, recording, and scanning without perm-ission in writing by the author.

While the advice and information in this book are believed to be true and accurate at the date of publication, neither the authors nor the editors nor the publisher can accept any legal responsibility for any errors or omissions that may be made. The publisher makes no warranty, express or implied, with respect to the material contained herein.

Printed on acid-free paper.

Printed in the United States of America
© 2020 by Konrad Christopher

Contents

Copyright i

Introducing the Apple MacBook Air (2020) 1

Use the Macbook Air like an Expert 3

Chapter 1

Setting User Accounts on MacBook Air 6

Administrator Account Set-up 7

Standard Account Set-up 9

Sharing Only and Guest Account 10

Chapter 2

Hidden Settings on MacBook Air 12

Shorter Routes on MacBook Using Mac Keyboard 18

Chapter 3

The Dock, System Preferences and Siri 24

The Dock on MacBook Air 24

Customizing Docks 25

The System Preferences on MacBook 28

The General Pane 30

The Dock Pane 30

Mission Control 32

Security and Privacy 33

The Display Pane 33

Siri on MacBook Air - "Hey Siri" 34

Chapter 4

Special Characters on MacBook Air 38

Keyboard Layout Setup 38

Keyboard Viewer 39

Key Combinations 40

Chapter 5

Launching your MacBook Air 42

Units Conversions with Spotlight 42

Keyboard shortcut for Spotlight 42

Screen Recording 44

Keyboard shortcut for screen recording 44

Screen recording with QuickTime Player 46

Recover Forgotten Passwords 47

Keychain Access 48

Chapter 6

Desktop and Application Management 50

Desktop Customization 50

Spaces and Mission Control 51

Managing Windows on Mac 53

App Management 55

Managing Files 55

Moving Files 56

Using Stacks 58

Chapter 7

Key Features on MacBook Air 59

The Notification Center 59

Launching Notification Center 59

Today Menu 60

Notification Menu 60

Do Not Disturb 61

The Menu Bar 61

Menus on the Menu Bar 62

Apple menu 62

Application menu 63

Status menus 63

Spotlight 64

Siri 64

Change the theme of the Menu Bar 65

Change the time and date on the Menu Bar 65

The Finder 66

Using Finder 67

The Sidebar 68

Searching for Files 68

Chapter 8

Launching an Application on Mac 70

Launch an App Using the Dock 70

Launch an App Using Spotlight 71

Launch an App Using the App Folder 72

Launch an App Using Launchpad 72

Closing an App 73

Installing an App 74

Uninstalling an App 74

Spotlight 74

Launching Spotlight 75

Searching on Spotlight 75

Chapter 9

Apps on the MacBook Air 77

Apps in the Dock 77

Other Apps on the Mac 80

Utilities on MacBook Air 83

App Store 85

Launching the App Store 86

Install an App from the App Store 87

v

Chapter 10

Touch ID on MacBook Air 88

Setting up Touch ID 88

Screen Time 89

True Tone 90

Night Shift 91

Chapter 11

Other Mac Features You Should Know 92

The Magic Keyboard 92

Function Keys 92

AirDrop 94

Sending and receiving contents through AirDrop 94

Trash 95

Right-Clicking 96

Option Click 97

Trackpad gesture 97

CONCLUSION: ENJOY YOUR MAC EXPERIENCE! 98

About the Author 99

Introducing the Apple MacBook Air (2020)

The Apple brand once again pulled one out of the top drawer to invent an astonishing MacBook tech that sure stands out from the rest of its competitors. The MacBook Air which was released late in March this year is one of the ultra-portable and inventive Macintosh Laptop series of the Apple brand. Apple has always been consistently a top tech puller as regards to the production of sleek laptops with high-speed operating and processing systems. Apple, this time has effortlessly brought a game-changing tenacity to the invention of the MacBook Air with demystifying features and software such as the handoff and the sidecar features.

Apple also ensured that the new MacBook Air was light-weighted as ever, with the brand rounding it with exquisite metallic body design. For most who love to use an on-the-go technology with beauty added to the craft, the 2020 MacBook Air makes it easy for mobile usage at any point. The laptop is sleek, durable, and crafty with its wedge-shaped design which Apple branded in its description of the gadget that it was "created from 100 percent recycled aluminium."

The new MacBook Air is also an ultramodern and powerful gadget for users, most especially Web and Software developers. It is incredibly portable and has a high-speed Mac Operating System with a 10th-generation Intel Processor of 1.1GHz dual-core Core i3. MacBook Air was also built with a custom-tailored superior keyboard which makes it a smart gadget for users. Among other upgraded features, MacBook Air possesses faster graphics (Intel Iris Plus) than its earlier models as well as an enhanced storage capacity which doubles the previously released Air models.

Apple has also added in the new MacBook Air a retina display which projects enhanced viewing angles scaling the last generation's Air; with pixels of over 4 million in the 13.3-inch screen display. It also has a long shelf battery life of more than 12 hours, with an in-built 54 watts-hour lithium polymer battery. For those who are frequent users of the Apple Mac brand, the MacBook Air is actually twice as fast the performance of preceding Air models. The 2020 MacBook Air model was configured with a quad-core processor and up to 16GB of Random Access Memory (RAM).

With the new 2020 MacBook Air reviewed and accessed, this book will be delving into the modalities of this new tech regarding its user set-up as well as unlocking some incredible features of the laptop. It will also shed more light on the functionalities the gadget delivers and equip you for a well-rounded user experience as you explore every inch of this new tech by Apple. For computer users who may have been accustomed to the Windows operating system, transition to the macOS may slightly take a bit ingenuity from you, however, the purpose of this book is to guide you through the processes from authentication down to operations.

Use the Macbook Air like an Expert

The MacBook Air 2020, just like every other MacBook will require a little adaptation skills from beginners or those who switched to MacOS. MacBook laptops in general are easy to adapt to and use. Right from the start up, set up and desktop, beginners will relish the experience of what it's like to own a MacBook. As a beginner using the MacBook Air, the size of the device will give you a thrilling experience which you will benefit from its portability and its incredible processor huge storage – although if you want a more powerful Mac, you might want to go for the Mac Pro series.

This is evident when running power-consuming programs on your Mac Air; you will get to hear the noise from the fan installed in the Mac. Nevertheless, macOS comes with special features such as the special keyboard functions and layout, Spotlight, App Store, Touch Bar – which is actually not on the Mac Air 2020 - and of course, Siri etc. These features and functions are things you can only find and are quite exclusive to Apple devices.

The first few things to do are customization and personalization. An interesting part of owning a Mac and every laptop and computer, is customization. Aside from the excitement from unboxing the Mac to booting up the system, nothing feels more jovial than setting up and customizing the MacBook.

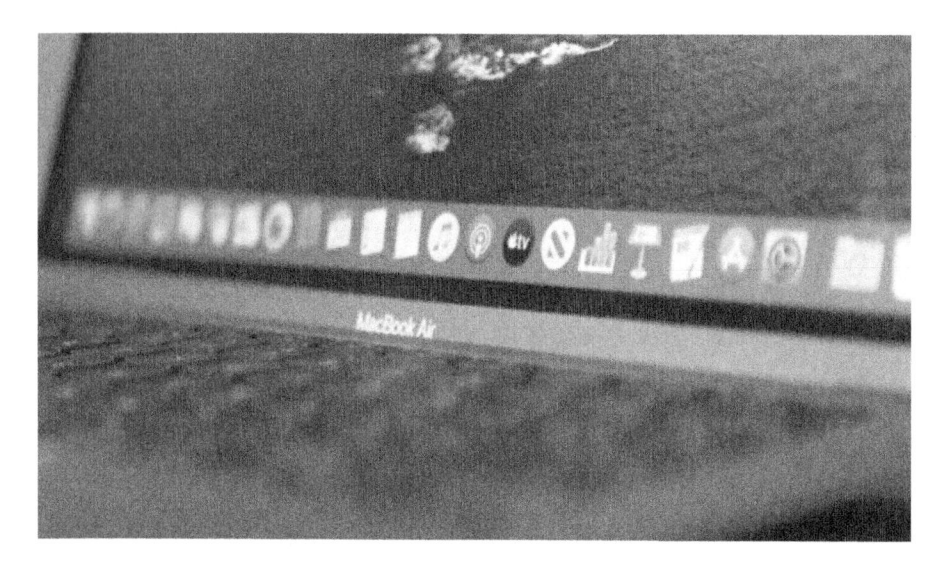

The Mac Air 2020 has a whole new set of keyboard – the "Magic Keyboard" as Apple calls it, with other changes in the Mac that sets it apart from previously released Mac Air and also MacBook in general too, right from the feel of the scissors mechanism of the keyboard which allows for more travel while typing to the inverted-T arrow keys then to the pixel packed Retina display. Understandably, most Mac users find it tedious and unappealing to use the Touch Bar, but the Mac Air 2020 uses the function keys just like the previous Mac Air versions. Therefore, if you are just switching from Windows to macOS with the Mac Air 2020, you do not need to worry about adapting to the seemingly stressful Touch Bar.

Nevertheless, to adapt and expertly use the MacBook Air, a few well-known tips below will put a buzz on your fingertips to help you make judicious use of your device. These tips are hints and effectively tested methods for efficient use of your Mac.

Chapter 1

Setting User Accounts on MacBook Air

As with every other computer, setting up the user account is the inaugural step in configuring the MacBook Air laptop. The user account allows you to pioneer and operate the gadget as well as take control of the inherent features it entails. Typically, every user of a computer, regardless of the brand, has to set up a user account to facilitate operational control. For the Apple brand, it is often quite a tricky first-start initiating this critical demand on the MacBook. Setting your Apple's User Account helps you to avoid issues such as dual-personalities on your operating system and invasion of privacy.

The user account majorly signifies ownership and unique, guarded rights over every feature on the computer and most essentially on the operating system. User accounts are created through sign-ups or domains on the computer (think of the way you create an electronic mail or a Facebook profile page through usernames and passwords). Setting a user account gives you authorization to the resources on the computer as well as authentication on the operating system. Users are potentially required to sign in to their accounts by validating their access to the system. The user would be requested to create certain credentials for the management of resources on the computer and other security purposes.

The MacBook Air user account is usually set up in different modes. For instance, a personal user has to set up the administrator account on Mac; which grants him the sole right to other accounts, which may be set up in standard and sharing modes. The idea here is that if you are setting up an individual account for your personal usage, then you would have to create one account on your Mac. Meanwhile, users who desire to share their Macs with other individuals can create multiple user accounts that grant access to those allowed to share control on the Mac. Of the multiple accounts, an administrator account is been set up to facilitate changes in the settings mode of the computer. Additionally, other accounts can be created as standard user accounts, which in this case, can also affect changes to the settings of the MacBook. Users who fancy accessing files on Mac over a network can also create sharing only accounts to effect changes to the features of their computer over external network sources.

Administrator Account Set-up

As earlier emphasized, the initial and unique account a user creates on the MacBook Air is the administrator account, which acts as an overseer to the system's settings as well as the creation of other accounts on the computer. The administrator facilitates crucial changes to the functionalities of the computer, which also includes altering other accounts of the computer and granting access to new users. It is also possible for the MacBook Air to possess more than one administrator account by enabling other users to become administrators.

The administrator account on your MacBook Air performs very 'top-secret' tasks on the system and as such caution should be applied when handing over an administrator account to just about anybody. Among other set-ups, the admin account is responsible for installing and updating software and applications and it provides access to deleting system files. You can also designate a primary admin account to a new administrator account for purposes such as troubleshooting and accessing other user files, but ensure that such an individual is a trusted ally in order to avoid security mishaps on your computer. The steps highlighted underneath will take you through the procedures in setting an administrator account.

> **System Preferences on Apple Menu**

From the newest and the updated version of the MacBook Air to the previous models, the process of activating a user account goes through the same procedure. Firstly, you click on the Apple icon or menu and select the **"System Preferences"** command located at the top left of your Mac screen to begin initiation. The system preference application is a detailed list of every setting on the MacBook, which provides access to a variety of panes on the workings of the laptops ranging from parental control down to software and the handling of internet accounts.

> **Users and Groups – Create User**

Once you have accessed the preferences, click on the **"Users and Group"** icon among the different panes that appear. This icon takes you straight to user privileges, which allow you to set up a new user account and personalize settings without affecting other users.

The next phase would be to access a new user by unlocking the lock icon on the bottom-left corner of the Mac Window. Click on the lock to kick-start this process and input your preferred administrator password. Your password must be unique and security proof. Ensure that the password tab is highlighted or you click on it. Next, you click on the "Unlock" icon in blue to continue.

Click on the plus sign (+) shown at the left sidebar and create an administrative account. You will be required to fill out your details including your name, password verification, and an optional password hint. Once your details are completed, click on the **"Create User"** icon to set up an administrator account for your MacBook. You can also create multiple users with this process. The Administrator account will be made available and accessible on the login screen of your Mac.

Standard Account Set-up

Unlike the administrator account, standard user accounts are only limited in their functionalities and access. Standard users only have limited access to system files and software changes. However, with this account, you can perform usual tasks on your MacBook such as personalizing your desktop and running software. This connotes that a standard user has guaranteed access to files contained in their home folders and can make changes to the settings in the System Preferences as regards to personal use of the Mac.

Creating a new standard account is almost synonymous with the procedure used in creating an administrator account. First, you click on the plus (+) sign after you must have gone through **"System Preferences"** and the **"User and Groups"**, then select **"Standard"** as the new account from the options displayed. You will then be required to fill out your details (user's full name and account name) and then enter a password, which will be verified twice. Click on **"Create User"**, and it automatically creates a new standard account on your Mac with a new home folder. The new user will be able to log in to the MacBook and access files.

Sharing Only and Guest Account

A Sharing Only Account on the Mac allows users to create alternative accounts for sharing folders and files on the device. In the event that you use your computer for file sharing, you can create accounts for users to only access specific files. To proceed with this setup, select **"Sharing Only"** from the account menu and fill out the information required.

On its part, the Guest Account only allows users to surf the device, while also restricting accesses to any important files or documents on the device. To set this up, select **"Guest User"** on the **"User & Groups"** preference pane and select the options required for a secondary user to access the computer. When a guest user uses the Mac, their files are immediately deleted when they log out.

Chapter 2

Hidden Settings on MacBook Air

The Macintosh Operating System has been designed by Apple to give users more invigorating computer experiences. The MacBook OS was instinctively polished by Apple for an enhanced and adaptable user experience and this is what marks it out from other operating systems. There are facets of your laptop that you could explore with hidden settings, which have been unearthed for this purpose. These settings have been aptly defined to allow you customize your experience of the Mac.

1. Digitally Append Signatures on PDF Documents

This feature has been handpicked because most Mac users aren't aware that they can digitally append signatures on their laptop with the webcam as an extension. You can sign any PDF document using the preview by selecting **Tools > Annotate > Signature > Manage Signature**. Once you select the **Manage Signature** option, hold up your signature (append on a paper or board) in front of the webcam and it automatically creates a digital signature that would be imprinted on the PDF. As the signature is created, you can drag and place it where you are required to sign.

2. Authenticate Mac with Apple Watch

For users who own an Apple Watch synchronized with their MacBook, unlocking your Mac device with the Watch gives you a more rapid access to your laptop than authenticating it manually. The Apple watch, besides unlocking your MacBook with the use of the touch ID or a passcode, also allows you to authenticate certain parts of the operating system. With your Apple Watch, simply double click the **side buttons** and it would let you into the system in a flash. It is an incredible feature and very convenient in unlocking your Mac computer.

If you have not synchronized the Apple Watch with your Mac, you will not be able to bypass the log-in screen with the Watch. To activate it, open the **System Preferences** menu and the select **Security and Privacy**. Under this menu, select **General** and check the box tagged **Allow your Apple Watch to unlock your Mac** while the Watch is on standby. This definitely would grant you access to authenticating your Mac with the Watch the next time you turn on your device.

3. **Concealing Location Service on Mac**

It is quite boggling that Personal Computers are adopting many features from mobile phones and the MacBook OS has not been any different either. The Location Service on your Mac is an enabled device that keeps track of your current location through Wi-Fi positioning and your laptop's Internet Protocol (IP) address. The Location Service on your device helps keep track of vital components like weather and maps within your location and for many it is an absolute necessity.

However, others may just want this feature disabled on their Mac for reasons that some applications on their device can access their locations. If you feel the need to conceal your location from these apps, open the **System Preferences** menu and select **Security and Privacy** from the options. While in this menu, click on **Privacy** and opt for **Location Services** and you will be presented with a number of apps that access your location. Deselect the apps and programs you don't want to use this service by unchecking the available boxes.

4. Access Emoji Keyboards

Similar to the iPhone Operating System, the MacOS has a built-in Emoji keyboard that gives you a face-time chatting experience. Most users have been accustomed to the Emoji keyboard on their mobile phones but most aren't aware that they can be accessed on the MacOS. You can activate the Emoji keyboard by pressing down the keys **Control + Command + Spacebar** at the same time and it would bring up the keyboard where you can select from your favorite emojis.

5. File Sharing Using iCloud

With the creation of an iCloud account, files and folders from your Mac can be shared to various contacts without any form of altercation. This feature operates with the MacOS and it allows you to easily send files to designated contacts within your operating system. To use this feature, locate the **Finder** on your Mac and then choose the file you wish to share to contacts. You would find the **Share** menu (an arrow out of a box) located at the top of the Finder Window; click on it and select **Add People** from the options available. Once this is done, the next dialog box can be used to alternate between the methods you wish to share the files as well the recipients of the file.

You can also enhance your use of the iCloud account by synchronizing various folders on your MacBook. Apple in the MacOS ensured that the cloud storage is packed with essential capacities to facilitate easy use for storing files. To sync desktop folders to iCloud, open the **System Preferences** menu and locate **iCloud**. Next you locate **Options** on the iCloud drive and select the folders or files you want to automatically synchronize to your cloud storage account.

6. Hide and Combine Apps Swiftly

As you may be aware, you can switch between applications by pressing the **Command Key** and hitting the **tab button** to switch between open apps. Meanwhile, you can actually hide or quit an open app as well from the tab menu. If you keep holding on the command key and land on a certain app and hit the **H** key, it will hide the app. The **Q** key while running this task will quit the app instantly.

The macOS also has in it a feature where you can combine app windows into various tabs more proficiently. This feature is similar to the way you create multiple tabs on a phone browser; you can also assemble app windows in the same vein. For certain Mac programs including Apple's developed apps like the Apple Maps or any app that supports the creation of multiple tabs, you can conveniently run this feature. Simply click the **Window** option visible at the top of the page and then select **Merge All Windows** to combine several windows in a tab series.

7. Free up space on the Hard Drive

The hard disk drive on your Mac is a high capacity and low cost device saddled with the responsibility of storing data from the operating system, documents and files and so on, on the long term basis. Now you would agree that a storage facility or drive can be overwhelmed or overloaded with excess data and may need a bit of freedom to ensure it is fit for purpose.

On your Mac, you can free up the hard drive easily when it runs low. Click on the **Apple Menu** on the top side of the screen and the select **"About This Mac"**. When the window to the option emanates, open the storage tab and click Manage to free up unnecessary space on the hard drive. More often than naught, cloud based files such as email attachments and iTunes files do not necessarily require local storage to encompass them. You can free them up by selecting the **Optimize** option on the particular window you are on.

8. Using Mac Dictator

The Mac Operating System has an in-built speech detecting feature called the Dictation. Instead of typing, just press the function key twice and the microphone icon will pop up and then you can start speaking into the microphone and it will type out what you dictate. When you have performed this, click **done** and it will save automatically.

9. Expand Files and Preview

Expanding a file on the Mac System also comes with its own niche. If you want to expand a file without fully opening it, you can simply press the **SpaceBar** or use the forestalled trackpad to expand it. Most users manually double click files and then keep clicking to open installed files. Howbeit, by clicking the **Space Bar** you can run a mini preview of any file and it makes navigating the file system a thousand times more efficient than having to open every file individually. For instance, if you want to launch a PDF, you can do more than just preview and mark it up without even opening it in with the native Mac preview app.

10. Altering Finder Windows on Mac

The finder is the default file manager used in all Macintosh devices to locate and organize files. It is located at the top section of the Mac screens and uses icons and windows to make contents of the Mac available to you. It also helps display contents from other storage devices as well as the iCloud Drive. Most times you may find the default appearance of the finder less appealing and may want to alter it. To initiate this, open the **View** menu in a new window at the top of the screen and select the **Show View Options.** The next window from here allows you to reset the size of the icons, texts, position of the Finder, as well as the grid spacing. Once this has been activated, the device will update the settings of all Finder Windows moving forward.

Shorter Routes on MacBook Using Mac Keyboard

For Mac users, life can be so much fascinating when they have to take shorter routes when initiating commands on their laptops. One of the best things about using a MacBook is Apples' integration of hardware and software and the best way to appreciate that integration is to learn the language of Mac keyboard shortcuts. There are various combinations on the MacBook that offer a user a much swifter and pragmatic experience on their gadgets. With the use of key combinations tested on the MacBook Air keyboards, you can entreat yourself to initiate commands without using a trackpad or mouse.

Keyboard shortcuts on MacBook Air are initiated by holding one or more modifier keys alongside the last key of the shortcut to complete the command. Keyboards and Menus on Mac are often marked by symbols depicted for certain keys, which also include the modifier keys for Mac Systems **(Shift, Control, Option, or Alt Key).**

Modifier key	Symbol
Command	⌘
Shift	⇧
Option	⌥
Control	⌃
Return	↩
Delete	⌫
Forward Delete	⌦
Up Arrow	↑
Down Arrow	↓

With these commands triggered on the MacBook Keyboards, your speed on the computer will greatly be fast-tracked. Shortcut techniques are easier ways of executing and navigating commands on your MacBook and they save you the stress of clicking your way through every execution. For instance, most Mac users who aren't accustomed to using shortcuts oftentimes highlight text using the mouse and then right-click "copy". While this command functions accurately on the computer, it is however maladroit and decelerates your work. Instead, you could just perform this task by simply holding the Command Key and C **[Command + C]**.

Left Arrow	←
Right Arrow	→
Page Up	⇞
Page Down	⇟
Top (Home)	↖
End	↘
Tab Right	→|
Tab Left	|←
Escape (Esc)	⎋

There are varieties of shortcut commands at Mac's disposal that you can initiate. The **Command Key**⌘ most of all is tantamount to the **Control Key** on a Windows PC but it performs handier tasks than the Control Key. Also, as a user, you can alternate between these shortcuts from software to specific applications to suit your penchant. Simply enter the **System Preferences** menu (the settings panel on the MacBook) and then find **Keyboard-Shortcuts** to change your shortcuts' preferences. Moving forward, the most important shortcut tool that you need to get abreast with you to relish your Mac experience will be highlighted in subsequent chapters.

Command ⌘ + Spacebar: Spotlight Search Field Shortcut

As aforementioned, the command key is an integral shortcut key on the Mac Operating System. The spotlight search field shortcut is initiated to find a file or an application on the Mac system from the finder window. To initiate this, press the ⌘ + **Spacebar** and the spotlight search tool will emerge. Using the shortcut, you can locate files that are harder to locate on the Mac and the results are usually provided instantaneously. The Spotlight Search Field also surfs through features such as bookmarks and text to files on the hard drive. This shortcut can also be used to launch **"SIRI"** – the Apple Voice Control Assistant – on the Mac Air.

Command ⌘ + M: Window Minimization

For most users who open numerous applications on their system, switching from one app to another can be tedious sometimes. This combination makes it easier to minimize the front app window to the dock. Simply hold both the **Command Key ⌘ and M** to initiate this shortcut. You can also minimize all windows, which belong to the front app by pressing the **Command key ⌘ + Option ⌥ + M.**

Command + Q: Shutting down Apps

Perhaps an application on your Mac needs shutting down; you can perform this task by simply clicking the **Command ⌘ + Q Key** to shut down the app completely. As opposed to using the **red X** button which is displayed at the top right of any application on the Mac, the best bit about this shortcut is that it doesn't just minimize the app but it shuts it down completely and stops it from running.

Command + Shift + 4: Screenshots on Mac

Taking screenshots on your MacBook Air is easier than it has ever been as opposed to the Windows PC where you would have to use snipping tools. To take a screenshot of an app window, just press the **Command + Shift + 4 Key** and then click **"Space"**. This shortcut cut tool puts the specific screenshot in rectangular cropped form and it comes very handily as regards taking a snippet of images or text on the internet. To take a screenshot of an app window without the shadow around it, just press **Command + Shift + 4 Keys + Space** and then press and hold option when you click the screenshot. By default, the Mac saves the screenshot to the desktop; however, to copy the screenshot to the clipboard, just hold the **Control Key** by taking the screenshot and it will be copied to the clipboard.

Option + F1 – F12: Quick Action Shortcuts

The **Function Keys (F1 – F12)** on the keyboards correspond to specific quick actions such as adjusting the volume and changing the brightness of the screen. This shortcut will allow you to directly launch the setting spin for the quick action that you want. Simply press **Option + the Function Key** that you want to launch the setting for. For instance, to launch the settings for the keyboard, press **Option⌥+ F5**. This takes you directly to the keyboard settings.

Command + Control + Q: Swift MacBook Lock

It is virtually very exhausting trying to lock your MacBook from the menu bar, but there is an easier and swift way to tackle this head on. Probably you are hurriedly prepping for an appointment and you want others snooping on your device, this command would help lock your MacBook in milliseconds. Simply press the ⌘ + ^ + **Q** and your MacBook Air would switch to the lock screen as soon as you initiate.

Chapter 3

The Dock, System Preferences and Siri

The Dock on MacBook Air

The Dock on your MacBook is a row of icons where all the features and applications are domicile and accessed. It is a small bar or panel which allows you to access applications, files and folders more swiftly without having to locate them in the system. The dock by default is resident at the bottom of the MacBook screen. When you first unleash your Mac, the dock might look a little bit confusing because it contains pre-existing icons for applications. Apple crowds the dock with icons they assume you may need or want to explore. However, to suit your preference you can customize the dock to alter its style or add features and applications.

This feature on the MacBook contains the application section on the left side of the screen, the Document/Window section on the right section and inclusively, the Trash bin on the far right. The Finder (a default File Manager on MacBook) and Trash icons are the only icons that are shielded from arrangement or dismissal on the dock as they are permanently locked in place.

The application section on the dock contains icons like the Dashboard and Finder. Once an application has been launched on your MacBook Air, a black dot will be displayed underneath to indicate that it is presently running. If an application does not have an icon on the dock but is launched by the user, it automatically appears on the dock as a running app. As the application closes, the icon disappears from the dock. It is also conceivable to allow an app stay in the dock permanently and there are two techniques you can adopt. Firstly, you can drag the application of your choice from the Finder into the dock. The second technique is to launch the application and as it runs, click **Control^ + the temporary icon and then click "Keep in Dock".** This will store the application on the dock for good.

On the other hand, the Document/Window Section contains file links and minimized windows. From the Finder, folders and files can be included into this section of the dock. Click on the Finder to open a window and then navigate to the file you wish to include, and then drag to the right section of the dock. An icon would be created to open the file or folder instantly from the dock. Windows also can be hidden from view and placed in the dock. Click the yellow circle with the [-] in the upper left corner of the window and it will appear on the dock. You can always restore the window by clicking on its icon.

Customizing Docks

As earlier emphasized, docks can be customized to suit the user's preference or style. You can alter the position, size and magnification of the dock.

1. **Customize the dock perfectly**

Depending on your preference and how you want the dock to be positioned or angled, you can fine-tune the entire setting of the dock. Start by launching the **System Preferences** and then click on "**Dock**". On the display of the next screen, you would have multiple options to configure and right in the dock is the ability to increase or decrease the size of the dock by dragging the **Size** slide either left or right. Next is the **Magnification** menu, which enables you to magnify the size of the icons when you move the cursor over the dock. You can minimize or maximize the size of the icon based on your preference. As earlier, emphasized, the dock by default is domicile on the bottom of the screen but if you find it a bit drift, you can position it on the left or right side of the screen.

There are other options to play around with in customizing the dock. First, you can enable **Show Indicators for Open Applications**. This makes it easier to find a running app on the dock. There is also a preference to **Automatically Hide and Show the Dock** or you can press the shortcut **Command + Option + D** to enable or disable it. You can also decide to hide recent apps on the Dock. Simply click on "**Show Recent Applications in Dock**" to alternate between the options to hide or show a running or recently launched application.

2. **Instantly Access Dock Preference**

You absolutely do not need to take a long route when you want to access the dock preference/settings. Simply right click the separating line on the dock and select **Dock**

Preferences and the **Menu** and you would automatically be directed to the dock settings.

3. Shortcut For Changing The Dock Position

Now you don't want a tedious route to changing the dock's position every time your tech buds pops up. Of course, you can alter the position of the dock from the preferences spot but there is a quick shortcut to do that almost instantaneously. Click on the separate line on the dock and hold it, press the Shift key and drag the dock to whatever position you want it (Left or Right).

4. Adding And Organizing Apps In The Dock

Organizing the applications allows you to identify and access your favorite or most used apps in the dock, more effortlessly. To perform this task, drag the app from the application folder or launch pad and place it in the dock. The frequently used to dragged app in the dock, right click on the app, select options in the menu, and choose **"Keep in Dock"**. Because you have to remove the app, simply drag it out of the dock to the launch pad or app folder. A spectacular way to categorize your applications on the dock is to ensure that they are placed in the right order.

5. Switch Between Two Recently Opened Apps

Switching back and forth between two recently opened applications on your Mac is straightforward. To alternate between two apps, press the **Option Key** and click on the **dock icon** to go back to the app you launched previously.

6. Adding Folder To The Dock

A folder that is frequently accessed can be added to the dock to create an easier route to reaching it. Rather than going all the way to the Finder to access the folder always, simply drag the folder from Finder or desktop and drop it on the dock. When you click on the folder, it will transform into a stack, allowing you to quickly access inherent files/folders. You can also customize the stack in fan, grid or list formats, depending on your preference.

7. Adding Website Shortcuts To Dock

There are many ways to access a website on your Mac but accessing a website through a shortcut on the dock is the fastest route to take. To add a website shortcut to the dock, simply click-hold the link on the address bar and drag down to the dock on the far right. The shortcut will be fashioned into a globe icon and from there you can access the website whenever you please.

The System Preferences on MacBook

The **System Preferences** menu is an application on the MacBook Air, which can be referred to as the 'MotherBoard' of a MacBook Laptop because it essentially provides routes to the control and adjustment of every setting on the device. The **System Preference** application, separated into diverse preferences panes, is the pathway you go through when the need to tweak or make changes to the features on the MacBook arises. Unlike other MacOS tools like the Terminal and Disk Utility domicile in the Utility folder, the **System Preferences** menu stays in the application folder but can be accessed easily from the Apple menu route on the top left of the Mac screen or from the dock, where it can also be launched when added. The **System Preferences** app on the dock is an icon, which looks exactly like a set of interlinked cogs. To add the **System Preferences** to the dock, click on **Command + Space bar** and type out *"System Preferences"*. Once it appears, drag the icon and drop it on the dock, from the search result.

The fastest way to access, the **System Preferences** is through the Apple menu route. Perhaps you don't fancy clicking all the way through to the application folder, simply click on the **Apple logo** on the top left of the Mac screen and select it from the menu. On the view menu on the top left, you have options that can organize the **System Preferences** alphabetically or categorically, depending on what you prefer. The panes on the System Preferences allow you to alter settings on any of the categories you select. It is an ecstatic way to modify your Mac on diverse aspects ranging from how the device functions to its appearance. Sometimes **System Preferences** have a whole set of levels or categories inside them. For instance, on the Keyboard pane, you would see a vertical list at the top (a list of tabs) where you can switch from keyboard preferences to text preferences, to shortcuts, input sources or dictation.

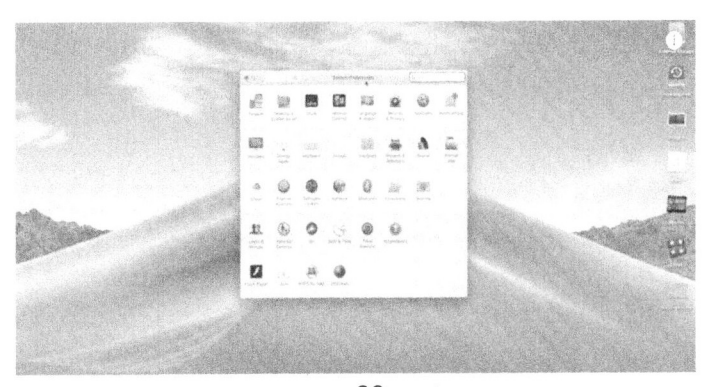

The General Pane

On the **General** pane, you will find a few system settings and you can alter them by selecting the drop down menus or the radio buttons or checkboxes. On this pane, you can adjust how the Mac functions. For example, if you want to change the default Safari web browser, click on the **"Default Web Browser"** option to switch from the Safari app to any browser of your choice, available or currently installed on the Mac.

The **General** pane also contains menus such as the appearances and highlighting colors, where you can change the appearance of the Mac from light view to dark view. Generally, on most of the System Preferences panes, you would find a question mark beneath which gives you a detailed description of each of the options on the panes. While on the **General** pane, if you want to go back to explore other system preferences, click on the **"Show All"** icon on the top of left of the screen.

The Dock Pane

On the dock, you can customize various options on the Mac such as the size, magnification, different options with the check boxes. Features and applications are kept in the dock for much easier access. The dock has been extensively emphasized in the previous chapter, however, a number of options on the dock settings have been highlighted below:

- **The Size** slider allows you to modify the size of the dock. If the dock is very full, it will not be able to get as big because it hits the sides of the screen.
- **The Magnification** slider allows you to modify the size that icons grow to when you hover your cursor over them.
- **The Position** on screen buttons determine where on the screen the dock sits: the left, bottom, or right edge of the screen.
- **Minimize windows** using: determines the minimize effect used when minimizing a window.
- **The double click a window's title bar to minimize checkbox** lets you minimize windows by double-clicking as well as using the minimize button.
- **The Minimize windows into application icon** prevent minimized applications from cluttering up the right side of the dock. Instead, right- or control-click the application to view its option menu and select the minimized item.
- **Animate opening applications** determines whether or not the icon bounces while the application opens.
- **Automatically hide and show the Dock** is a setting that hides the dock until the cursor is moved over it.
- **Show indicator lights for open applications** determines whether or not open applications have a visible indicator such as this

Mission Control

In similar fashion, we have mission control, which is used to show all of your apps in a specific layout. When the apps are all open, you can use this feature to spread your applications all out and show them in smaller screens. For instance, when you open the Safari web on your computer, and hit the mission control button, it spreads both of them partly so you can see the different applications you have open.

If you have multiple desktops, you can scroll to the top to view them. Probably you want a new desktop you can **click** + to create one and move the Safari web over to the second desktop. This feature allows you to slide in between desktops mostly using the trackpad device. In the **Systems Preferences** pane, you can customize the **Mission Control** feature via the hot corners' menu on the bottom left.

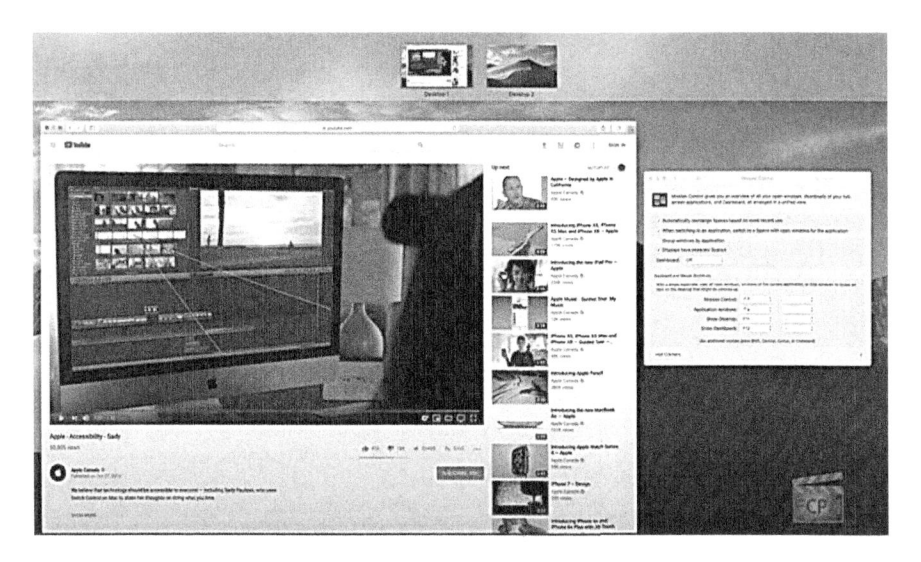

Security and Privacy

Security and Privacy on the Mac system is an essential feature that ensures the safety of almost every facet of your computer. On this pane, you have features on the Mac that are locked out until you input a password to unlock them. For your device to make these alterations, click on the **lock icon** on the bottom left and you will be requested to verify your account by signing in. Once it's unlocked you can make changes on the Mac. On the **Security** pane also, you can adjust plug-ins on other apps on the device with unverified developers from the **App Store**. You can allow these apps to operate on the security pane and be fully functional. Furthermore, there are features like **"file vault"** which is the encryption for your computer and you can customize the **"firewall"** if you have it enabled.

Privacy on the other hand is where you can set and reset specific apps, for instance the microphone, location services, full disk access and the likes. You can disable what apps have access to features on your device.

The Display Pane

The **Display System Preference Tab** is more hardware related than the afore-described panes. Users who have multiple displays on their Mac device can initiate commands to add a second preference pane over on the other display. You can customize each one of your displays ranging from brightness, resolution and alter the control panel of each of those displays. The other option on this tab is the **Airplay Display, which** allows airplay over an Apple TV.

You can also construct **Arrangement** if you have multiple displays. If there are more than two displays in your computer, the arrangement tab is where you alter any of the displays to make them secondary. This ensures that when you drag a window from one side to another, it actually goes over to the other display. On the display pane you can also calibrate and set profiles for the color scheme or temperature on your Mac.

Siri on MacBook Air - "Hey Siri"

On the MacBook Air, Siri is a Personal Assistant that runs simple errands on your device. The Apple Operating Systems in this prime age have not just made Siri a Voice Assistant but has enhanced this technology to become an instinctive Artificial Intelligence (AI) system that performs ultra-activities on the MacBook with simple vocal commands uttered to it. Apple, making the virtual assistant very competitive, integrated it on every MacBook OS and IOS platform.

Siri is orchestrated to perform very handy tasks on the Mac System ranging from maximizing features like Music and Maps, to the Calendar app, Weather and Messages. You can activate Siri to perform tasks on your device through voice instructions by just saying **"Hey Siri"** accompanied by a command you want to initiate. Siri comes in very valuable on your Mac because it lifts the burden of clicking through every command or typing out keywords on a web search. For instance, Siri can be ordered to perform a search task on the web or identify a specific location. Siri is somewhat similar to the virtual Google Assistant but it's very much versatile and has been upgraded by Apple recently on the newest MacBook Operating Systems.

One of the best things about Siri is that it is very accustomed to natural languages and it's not restricted by accent of any kind, as long as the commands requested are uttered in the English Language. Siri is also a very funny character that offers numerous pre-programmed responses to amusing questions. This author once asked Siri what its name meant, it replied that it was "a riddle wrapped in an enigma, tied with a pretty ribbon of obfuscation."

To create a **Dictation Command** and activate Siri using the **"Hey Siri"** catchphrase, follow these steps:

1. Open the **System Preferences** pane and click on the **Keyboard** icon and next select **Dictation**, Turn the dictation on and enable the enhanced dictation command.
2. Next, you select **Accessibility**. Select dictation and enable the dictation keyword phrase. In this field, you type "**Hey**" – this is the dictation to call before the command name.
3. Enable the **Advanced Command** checkbox on dictation command. Enter the admin password and click on the plus + sign to create a new command – the command name will be "Siri". Note that whenever you are using an application on the Mac, it will open the Siri application. You can choose **Open Finder Items** on the **Perform** option and select the "**Siri App**" from the Applications Folder and click '**Done**' to confirm.

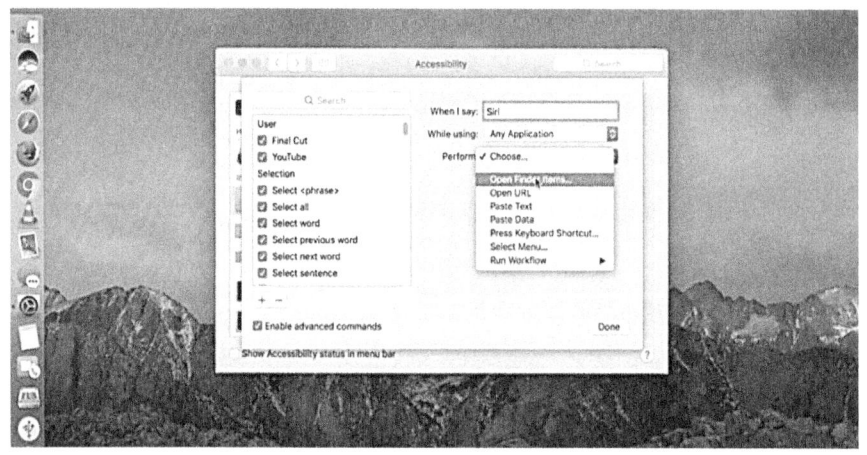

You can enable the "Listen for **"Hey Siri"** option in the **Siri** pane of **System Preferences.**

1. Select the **System Preferences** option from the Apple Menu

2. On the preferences pane you would see the Siri preference panel at the bottom. Click on it and then select the box that enables **'Listen for "Hey Siri"'**
3. To initiate the **"Hey Siri"** setup, click on the **"Continue"** tab to begin the process
4. Next would be the verbal setup process where you would be required repeatedly site commands displayed on the screen. For example, a command like *"Hey Siri, open the documents folder"* will be provided for you to recite.
5. When this process is completed, click on **'Done'** and close the preferences panel.

Chapter 4

Special Characters on MacBook Air

Before inputting special characters on the MacBook Air, a keyboard type should be entered for use in the future. Every Macintosh keyboard comes with an added difference to enable fast input for the different languages. This means that the keyboard layout is different for different languages. These differences help users to type faster. For example, a Spanish typist would prefer alphabets with accents or symbols placed in a more accessible position. Special characters include symbols, currency signs, emojis and many other characters, basically every character aside from A to Z and 1 to 0. For English speakers, the American and British keyboards also have different layouts.

Keyboard Layout Setup

> ➤ Select the **Apple menu** on the menu bar.

> Click **System Preferences.**

> Then switch to **Input Sources** on the row of tabs.
> Click the + sign by the left.
> Click on your **Preferred Language.**
> Then click **Add**.
> Tick the **Show Input** menu in menu bar if it is not ticked.
> A flag icon appears at the top of the screen.
> Click your preferred **Flag** icon and again choose your **Preferred Language**.

Keyboard Viewer

For beginners, it is best to know that to see the special character on the MacBook Air; an option is made available for the special characters. To access the special characters, use the Keyboard Viewer; go to **System Preferences > Keyboard** and tick the Show keyboard and Emoji Viewers in the menu bar.

A display simulation appears and shows all the special characters. This reveals the special character hidden in a key. The default keyboard shortcut for the various special characters could also be modified. The keyboard shortcut is **Control + Command + Space.** A categorized display of all the special characters appears on the screen. This ranges from emojis, bullets, math symbols, punctuations and a lot more characters.

Key Combinations

Across the second row of the Mac Air 2020, some frequently used special characters are positioned for faster input. They can be used using special keys. To use the special characters, keyboard shortcuts become very useful and they are accessed using key combinations. In this case, Hold and Press the required keys and release them at the same time. The following are some special keys that are frequently used in keyboard combinations:

- Cmd (Command) ⌘
- Ctrl (Control) ^
- Esc (Escape)
- Fn
- Shift ⇧
- Option ⌥

When these keys are entered together with the right combination, special characters display on the screen. For example, to type the "@" character on your device, enter this key combination **Shift + 2.**

These special characters also have character accents. Even most beginners don't know that emojis can be found on Mac as well as character accents. In a situation where accent marks are needed on characters; hold and press the character; a menu pops up with the variety of accents available on the character. Understandably, not all characters have accent marks.

Chapter 5

Launching your MacBook Air

On opening the newly purchased MacBook Air, lift the lid to boot it up. The Mac Air 2020 launches automatically when you open the lid. Apple has since removed the power button and replaced it with the Touch ID, which is more secure.

The Touch ID acts as the power button and it is a powerful key that does more than switching on your Mac. The Touch ID is the black button on the right end of the first row on the Mac Air 2020; it is right above the Delete key. If the lid of the Mac is open but the Mac is off, press the Touch ID to turn it on. The Mac Air also wakes up when the lid is open and it is connected to a power source.

Units Conversions with Spotlight

Spotlight is used for searching for files, documents and locating items on Mac. It is found at the top right corner on the menu bar and has a 'magnifying glass' icon which is popularly understood to be a search icon.

Keyboard shortcut for Spotlight

If you are faster with the keyboard, the keyboard shortcut for Spotlight is **Command + Space.** But there's more to Spotlight than just searching for documents or files and locating items in the laptop.

If you are just switching from Windows to Mac, you might not know that Spotlight has additional features which can help you do little things that might boggle your mind, such as; currency conversions, converting from millimeters to inches, checking up words with dictionary results and yes, math- for quick calculations and humongous numbers arithmetic that bewilder your mind.

Converting from one unit to another unit on Spotlight is very easy:

- Press **Command** + **Space** and a search field appears on the screen

- On the search field, type in the unit you want to convert and **Spotlight** gives you instant results the moment you are typing.

If you want to convert $1 to other currencies just type 1 USD and the results appear with more suggestions of other currencies' equivalent. If you want to find the equivalent value of a Dollar to Australian Dollar; you could also type $1 to AUD.

Although, finding exchange rates on Spotlight will require you to input the currency abbreviation of the currency or better still, using the currency's sign. This also applies to converting temperatures, measurements etc. If you love using Siri, you might as well say the words and get the conversion results instantly.

Screen Recording

It is 2020 and making screen records have become common, not just on Macs but on iPhone and pretty much every Smartphone being released this era. From taking selfies, recording videos, taking snapshots to screen recording and even screen recording while recording a video. Cool, right?

Screen recordings have gone so viral that sometimes we forget that they are informal records and amateur clips. Howbeit, as far as they do what we need them to do, then they are good enough and quite important depending on the content they carry. However, with further editing, the difference will be classes apart.

Screen records are the best ways of showing a person who is not actually present how exactly to do something on their laptop. They are best for tutorials too. Perhaps you want to have the clip of a particular moment in a movie. You want to capture a particular moment happening on the screen of your MacBook; then screen recording is the best way to go about it.

Keyboard shortcut for screen recording

Since 2018 screen recording became faster with the introduction of MacOS Mojave. You can record the entire screen of your Mac or record a preferred portion of the screen.

- Press **Shift + Command + 5** and a control bar will appear. The first three icons on the control bar are designed by Apple to take screenshots of the window.
- You could choose to record the entire screen of your Mac or you could record a selected portion of the screen. If you do select to record only a portion of the screen, you could also crop and drag the selected portion.
- On the control bar, there is an option where the settings of the screen record can be changed. Click **Option** if you want to change the default save-to location, the timer, default selection, audio and microphone type (external, internal or none) etc.
- After selecting your choice, click on **Record** to begin recording and a Stop icon appears at the top right corner on the menu bar. This is the main hint that the recording has begun.
- To stop recording, click on the Stop icon or press **Command + Control + Escape.** A thumbnail of the videos appears after every recording at the bottom right corner of the screen. Click on the **thumbnail** to further edit the video.

After successfully recording a video on your Mac Air, a thumbnail appears only for a short time. If you feel no need to check the video, you may move on with other tasks as the video will automatically be saved. To do more or take a look at the video, click on the **thumbnail**. To edit and trim the video, click on **Trim**, which is next to the **Done, Delete** and

Share buttons. Click the **Done** button to save the changes on the video.

Screen recording with QuickTime Player

Apparently, other screen recording applications can be used for screen recording. There is a lot of software that can be used to capture the actions going on in your screen. **QuickTime** player is a multimedia framework developed by Apple in 1991. It can be used for different media formats. It can also be used for screen recording and editing.

- On your MacBook Air, right click on **QuickTime Player** in the Dock.
- Click on **New Screen Recording** on the menu.
- If it is not in the **Dock**, locate it using **Spotlight** and open it.
- Click **File > New Screen Recording.**
- A screen recording control box appears with a record button and a white arrow. Click on the white downward arrow for more options to change the recording settings. You may want to use an external microphone or headphone other than the default inbuilt microphone, then you can find the setting by clicking on the white arrow. Also, select **Show Mouse Clicks** in recording if you want your cursor to be surrounded by a black circle while clicking during recording.
- Next, you have to pick the portion of screen to record. Click on the **red record button** and then click

anywhere on your screen to begin recording if you want to record the entire screen.
- ➤ Otherwise, to record a selected portion, click the red record button and drag the appearing marquee to the desired area of recording and click **Start Recording, which** is in the desired area. And it begins recording. A highlighted shaded area surrounds your desired area. To remove the shaded area, press the **Escape key.**
- ➤ Click **Stop Recording** in the menu bar or press **Command + Control + Escape** to end the recording. In the dock, right click on the QuickTime Player and select Stop Recording in the menu. The video appears with an untitled name.
- ➤ You can **edit** and **save** the screen record.

Recover Forgotten Passwords

On the Mac Air, you are bound to do a lot of things which the laptop is definitely capable of running and handling. This goes from basically watching movies to playing games; the MacBook Air 2020 in its small size is a powerhouse. Within that time of usage, surfing the net is a daily bustle.

Apple makes everything from their software to their hardware, which is why it is compact and astute security-wise. But a slight challenge we tend to encounter while using the Mac is when we forget the password of a program or the login password to a website. However, Apple has that covered for a long time running now.

Have you ever tried to put in the login details to a website, only for some autofill to fill up the details for you, which sometimes can lead you to losing memory of the login details? This means that with auto fill, your passwords are being stored up somewhere, somehow in your Mac.

This is where **Keychain Access** comes in. Apparently, these days it has become easier to keep track of the number of followers one has on Twitter than to keep track of the numerous numbers of websites one has logged into. Remembering the password for the various websites is too much to handle and a lot to remember.

Keychain Access

Keychain Access is an Apple owned password management software. It helps store passwords, usernames, certificates, secure notes and makes user accounts secure. It is pre-installed in the MacBook Air. Here is how to get the forgotten password of any application or website on your MacBook:

- Open **Application folder** > **Utility folder** > **Keychain Access**. Alternatively, you use the Spotlight shortcut; **Command + Space** on the keyboard, then search for **Keychain Access** and open the application.
- At the bottom left corner on the screen, click **Passwords**, under the category section.
- Use the search bar at the top right corner and type the name of the program or website you need and search for it.

- When it appears, double click it on the program or website.
- A window with two tabs appears. Under the Attributes tab, an entry of the account is displayed including the username, URL, password, etc.
- At the end of the window, check or tick the Show **Password box** to reveal the password of the account.
- Another window will prompt you to enter the password of your MacBook Air. Enter the admin password of the MacBook.
- Having done that, the previous window will reappear revealing the password. Take a note of it and ensure it is secure then exit the Keychain Access.

In most cases, password managers are very useful. You could also use this tip to find the password of the Wi-Fi on your Mac.

Chapter 6

Desktop and Application Management

After logging in to your MacBook Air, it takes you to the desktop, which is pretty much the home screen in this case. The desktop is the space between the menu bar at the top and the Dock at the bottom. Whenever an application is launched, a window of the application appears on this desktop. If you are reading an article on the internet or you are watching a movie on QuickTime play, or you are surfing through some files on your Mac; they are all done on the desktop. Every window you open on a Mac appears on the desktop.

Desktop Customization

On launching your MacBook for the first time, at the set up, users are allowed to choose between a light appearance and a dark appearance for your desktop. For instance, you may want to change the Mac appearance or the desktop picture. You may also prefer solid colors for your desktop, or better still, effect the use of dynamic images. To enable these alterations, locate the desktop settings and follow these steps:

- ➢ Click the **Apple menu** and select **System Preferences.**
- ➢ Click **Desktop & Screen Saver** and select the Desktop tab.
- ➢ Down by the left is a set of triangles pointing to the various available folders containing your pictures, desktop images and solid colors. To include a folder to the desktop, use the (+) button.
- ➢ On the right, samples of all the pictures are displayed and ready to be used. You may navigate and click on your preferred picture to have it as your desktop picture. You may use a quality or larger image to suit your screen size in order to avoid blurry pictures.
- ➢ Check the Change picture box to use all the pictures in a folder. Tick the **Random order** box to have the images switching in random. You can change the timing of the pictures by clicking on the box next to the change picture box.

Spaces and Mission Control

There is only so much Mac users can do on a laptop at a time but then it becomes hectic managing the various windows open at the same time on the desktop. On the Mac Air, the desktop becomes really clustered with so many cramped windows opened. On windows, however, it is very easy managing all the windows opened on the desktop.

Apple thought of a way to easily organize the desktop and came up with **Spaces**. This is like having multiple desktops but on one monitor. Some Mac users do not know how useful this is on their device. With **Mission Control,** you can control and organize every window currently running on your MacBook.

- Press the **Functions Key F3** or use the keyboard combination **Control + Up** to open **Mission Control**. You could also swipe up three or four fingers on your trackpad to open Mission Control depending on the trackpad settings.
- At the top of the screen, the **Spaces bar** appears with a large + button at the end of the bar.
- Thumbnails of all the desktops are shown on the bar. Click on the thumbnail of the desktop you want to enter.
- Click the + button to add more desktops or spaces. To delete a space, hover about the space and click the × button. If the space contains some windows, then the windows are moved to another space.
- You can navigate between spaces in different ways. Open Mission Control and click on the space you want to switch into easily. On the trackpad, swipe left or swipe right with three or four fingers to navigate between spaces. Then on the keyboard use **Control + Left** to move left and **Control + Right** to move right.

With the Control, you could go to any specific space by simply pressing the control key and the space number. For example, the **Control + 1** combination takes you to the first space.

➢ It is quite easy to organize the desktop using Mission Control. You could classify every application you use on your Mac into different spaces or desktops. This is also helpful if you want to work with related windows in a particular desktop or move a window to a particularly preferred space in different ways:

➢ You can drag the window and then move it to the edge of the screen. This moves to the next space. Keep dragging the window until you get it into your preferred space.

➢ Right from the space, you have the window you want to move, enter **Mission Control**. Then you can drag the window you want to move to the displayed spaces on the Space bar at the top where your preferred space can also be found.

➢ If you want to have a particular application to always open on a specific desktop. **Right-click the icon** of the app in the Dock, select the **Options** menu and click on either of the **sub-menus**, which allows you to also assign the app to all desktop, or none at all.

Managing Windows on Mac

For every Mac beginner or anyone who switched recently to Mac, it is common to see some eye-catching buttons on every window without knowing what their functions are. At the top of every window on Mac, there are three round buttons that are similar to a traffic light. Yes, they are also called the **Traffic Light buttons** with regards to their color.

Red Button: The **Red button** closes or shuts down the application running a window and the window disappears. Hit **Command + W** to quickly close a window on the keyboard. When you press the **Yellow button**, the window also disappears. But it still runs in the background, it just does not show on the desktop.

Yellow Button: The **Yellow button** removes the window from the desktop and minimizes it back to the Dock without shutting down the application. The application can also be restored without the need to launch the application again. Users can continue from they stopped with nothing unchanged.

Green Button: Click on the Green button to have the window in full screen. When in full screen, the menu bar and Dock are removed from the screen and the application covers the entire screen. Also press the **Green button** to maximize or minimize the window to its standard size. Click and hold the **Green button** for more windows options.

Windows can also be dragged or moved, aligned and resized. To quickly switch between active windows, press **Command + Tab.**

App Management

In the world of PCs, a computer is only as useful and powerful as the software and apps installed on the computer. These days, manufacturers would want buyers to have something and maybe the necessary apps to start with when they get a new computer. This is the case with every operating system. Each operating system - like the MacOS - has quite a number of good inbuilt software and applications.

The MacBook Air comes with a lot of already installed apps. Some of which are well branded and owned by Apple. Your favorite will likely be in the Dock, which is located at the bottom of your screen. The Dock is the fastest way to open these apps.

You can add apps to the Dock by dragging it on the screen and dropping it in the Dock. You could also remove apps from the Dock by dragging the app out of the Dock. Dragging an app into the Trash does not mean that it is not permanently removed from your Mac. You can still access it from the Applications folder, or use either of Spotlight, LaunchPad or Finder to access it again. The Trash can be found in the Dock because it is something you will most like use often.

Managing Files

Files and documents have become very significant aspects of computer usage. This is why we need to know how to arrange and organize our files. The file management app on the Mac Air is similar to the File Explorer on Windows, if you are familiar with apps on Windows. The Finder is an app that helps to locate files and items on your Mac. It can also be used to quickly organize, move, duplicate and remove files on your Mac.

Files and folders

You can easily create folders on the Finder or even on the desktop. From the top right corner on the bar, simply click **File > New Folder** and enter the name of the folder. Press **Shift + Command + N** for keyboard enthusiasts. You can drag any item and put it into the new folder.

It is easy to move more than one item of file into the new folder. Select the files you want to move or **press Command + A** to select all items and drag one of the selected items into the new folder.

- If you want items to appear in a certain order, click **View > Sort By** to change the sorting of items listed on your Mac.

- To add tags to files click the **Finder icon** and find the file you need. Control click on the file and the tag setup appears on the screen. This way, it is easier to locate files because of the tags. They appear faster in search results.

Moving Files

Moving or duplicating files from one directory to any is sometimes not easy. To easily move a file from one place to another:

- Create a new tab on Finder. This allows you to duplicate tabs to enhance easy navigation. It is like opening two or more windows of File Explorer on a Windows computer.
- Open the Finder app and then select **File > New Tab** and a second tab is opened on Finder. Alternatively, you can also press **Command + T**. This way you could copy and paste files between folders. Here you can move items or files by having the preferred folder opened or active on the second tab and then on the first tab drag the item and drop it onto the second tab. A tab is different from a window. When you open a new tab in Finder, the new tab is opened in that same active window.
- To copy a file, select the file and click **Edit > Copy** visible on the top bar. Move to the location you want to copy the file and click **Edit > Paste**.
- Select an item, hold the **Option key** and drag the item into a preferred folder and release. You can copy a file using keyboard shortcuts **Command + C** for coping, **Command + V** for pasting and **Command + X** to cut a file.
- Duplicating a file is easy on Mac. Select the file, press **Command + D** and a duplicate of the file is created in the same folder. You could also select the file and click **File > Duplicate** to achieve the same result.
- Delete a file by selecting the file and pressing **Command + Delete**. You could also easily move it to the **Trash**.

- ➢ Find out the items or files on your clipboard by pressing **Edit > Show Clipboard.** This shows a list of previously cut or copied items.

Using Stacks

On the desktop, Mac users tend to have a lot of files and documents displayed unorganized on their desktop. Organizing these files might seem like a lot of work if you like having most of your files on the desktop screen. Stacks can be used to group these files depending on the type of file it is. You can group photos in one folder and still group documents in another folder.

- ➢ Click **View > Use Stacks** which is on the menu bar to use stacks or press **Command + Control + 0** on the keyboard.
  - ➢ Press **View > Group Stacks** By to change how stacks should be grouped.
  - ➢ Click **View > Show View Options** to modify the icon. You can use this to change the general thumbnail size of items in a folder.

Chapter 7

Key Features on MacBook Air

The Notification Center

When you get a notification, it is stacked in the Notification Center. The Notification Center holds all incoming alerts and notifications. It is a great feature on the MacBook Air, which is used to hide or turn notifications on or off. Notification Center can be accessed from anywhere without interrupting any ongoing activity.

Launching Notification Center

Open or launch Notification Center by clicking the Notification Center icon which is on far out on the end of the menu bar at the top right corner. The icon is a stack of three black dotted lines. Using a trackpad, swipe left with two fingers.

Notification Center slides out from the right and takes up a part of the right side of the screen. It appears with two sections; **Today** and **Notifications**. In the **Today** section, you will find widgets and tabs of events, today's weather and time etc. Click the Notifications tab to get to see all the notifications you have on your Mac.

Today Menu

Using the **Today Menu** is great for quickly checking on the events you have and changing or adding to your schedule and many more. It allows you to use widgets and as much as you want. If you enjoy using widgets on iOS or any other Smartphone, then you will enjoy using them on your Mac.

You can add widgets to the **Today** tab by scrolling down to the end of the tab and click Edit. A variety of widgets are available there. To get more widgets, go to the App Store and download more. Adding widgets is easy. A plus sign + is inscribed on a green circle while a minus – sign is inscribed on a red circle. They are used for adding or removing widgets.

Notification Menu

When you are in the Notifications section, you will find a long list of notifications and alerts that you have received including the ones you might have missed which could span weeks.

> ➢ Click on a **notification** to view it. This takes you to the app that sent the notification. On clicking the **notification**, it is removed from the Notification Center.
> ➢ If you do not want to bother yourself about opening a notification, then simply close it. Hover on top of the notification's tab and click the × at the top right corner.

➢ Clear all the notifications received on a particular day by clicking on the × sign on the right side of that day's date.

➢ You may want to disallow or allow nonfictions for some apps. Alternatively, you may want to change the style of alerts from an app and make the alerts visible when the screen is on locked. Select the **Apple menu** on the menu bar and go to **System Preferences > Notifications**. A lot of notification features can be changed in there for any app.

Do Not Disturb

When this is turned on, your Mac will show any alert or notification received. Alerts will be hidden, notification sounds will be turned off depending on the setting and incoming calls will be silenced. Open **Notification Center** and click on the **toggle switch** to turn on or turn off **Do Not Disturb.**

There is a faster way of turning on **Do Not Disturb** which you will find helpful. To quickly turn on **Do Not Disturb**, hold the **Command key and click on the Notification Center icon right on the menu bar**. This is an easy and fast way of turning on the **Do Not Disturb** tab without actually opening Notification Center on your device.

The Menu Bar

On every PC you come across, a menu bar is very handy and abetting. A menu bar helps to ease navigation and as the name suggests, it contains various menus and it offers more options to you. On every app and window, you are most likely to see a menu bar, like a strip across the screen tapered at the top. Except the app or window is on full screen, this feature will be available.

The menu bar consists of options and submenus that will help you get more from an app. Do you want to change the settings of an app onscreen or do you want to know more information about an app and you do not know how to go about it? Then the first thing to do is to look for the menu bar which is usually found at the upper end of the screen on every window.

The menu bar is a set of icons and menus at the top of the screen on the desktop of your MacBook Air. It is a really important feature on macOS and it is good for performing tasks quickly and using more app functions. On the menu bar, you will find the Apple menu – the one with an icon of the Apple logo – and a set of menus called App menus all on the left side of the menu bar. While on the right side of the menu bar, you will find the status menus, Spotlight and Siri icons for fast access etc.

Menus on the Menu Bar

Apple menu

The Apple menu is the first menu and icon on the menu bar, moving from the left down on the far end at the top of the screen. When you click the Apple menu, you will find important features, tools, commands and submenus such as System Preferences, App store, commands to lock your screen and finding more information about your Mac. It also has shortcuts to either shut down or to restart your Mac. You can also log out of your account or put your Mac to sleep on the Apple menu.

Application menu

Right after the Apple menu are the App menus. The App menus are a category of menus and commands that become handy when using an app or program on your Mac. Although some menus, commands or submenus may be different or not available on some apps depending on the kind of app you are using at that moment

On the desktop screen, you will also be able to use some of the functions on the App menus to perform some tasks. Right on the App menus, you will find the following menus; Files, Edit, View, Window, and Help. When an app or window is open, you will also find these App menus available for use with the name of the app appearing right before the menus. These menus consist of commands you will be in frequent need of on your device.

Status menus

Away on the right side of the menu bar, after the App menu are the status menus. The status menus are usually found to be icons and widgets – which could serve as an onscreen reminder. The status menus are often used to check up on the status of a system. Like on a Smartphone, you can check the date, time, your Mac's battery status or your Wi-Fi status from the top of your screen.

The status menus can be used for more than just checking your Mac's system status. You can turn your Wi-Fi on or off; you can add widgets from the App store and add it to the status menus. You could also use a volume icon to control the volume of your Mac from the status menus. Having your status menus in a particular order is easy. Simply hold the Command key and drag each icon into a preferred position. Also hold the Command key while dragging an icon out of the menu bar to remove it from the status menus.

Spotlight

Spotlight is one of Apple's most used features on MacOS; which is why there are many different ways of opening Spotlight. Spotlight can easily be accessed from the menu bar. You will find it after the status menus with a search icon on the right side of the screen. To quickly search for an app on your Mac, click on the search icon on the menu bar. If you do find keyboard shortcuts to be much faster or quicker than to click on a mouse or use a trackpad, then press **Command + Space** to open Spotlight.

Siri

Siri is a special feature which you will find on major Apple devices. It is the icon after the Spotlight icon on the menu bar. Siri is a device assistant which you can speak with to operate your Mac. Siri can do a lot from opening files, launching apps to making internet searches and many more.

Notification Center

To the right end of the menu bar is the Notification Center. It is the icon with the three dotted stacked lines. When you click on the Notification Center icon on the menu bar; a panel swipes out from the right side of the screen. The Notification Center is a quick way to look up your schedules and review notifications you have received. It can also be used to search through notifications you might have missed while you were away from your Mac etc. Hold **Option** and click on the icon to turn on **Do Not Disturb**.

Change the theme of the Menu Bar

You can change the theme of your menu bar to a dark theme.

- ➢ Click the **Apple menu** > **System Preferences** and select **General**.
- ➢ Choose **Use dark menu bar** and **Dock**.

Change the time and date on the Menu Bar

The time and date of your Mac is set automatically and the time zone is also set automatically using your current location. But you can manually change the time or time zone of your Mac.

- ➢ On the menu bar, click on the **date and time** on the status menus.

- ➢ A menu pops out, select **Open Date & Time Preferences.**
- ➢ A window with three tabs appears; select the **Date & Time tab**.
- ➢ To make changes to the date and time, click on the lock at the bottom of the window. You will be required to enter your administrator password. Click **Unlock** when you are done.
- ➢ Un-tick the **Set date and time automatically** box and change the date and time.

Follow this same process to either change the time zone or to change the date and time widget on the other two tabs.

Hide menu bar

An auto-hide feature is available for hiding the menu bar. The menu bar is usually hidden when on full screen. But you can have the menu to show up whenever you want. Click **Apple menu > System Preferences** > General and check the "**Automatically hide and show the menu bar**" option. To access the menu bar, hover your cursor and at the top of the screen and the menu bar appears.

The Finder

Finder is Apple's own unique file manager. When you turn on your Mac, it is automatically open. Finder goes beyond finding and organizing files. It is an important inbuilt app that can be used to navigate your MacBook. If you are just switching from Windows, you will discover that Finder is similar to File Explorer and it is also user friendly. Finder is the central app on the MacBook Air and literally every other Mac.

Using Finder

You can begin using Finder by clicking on its icon in the **Dock**. When you open a Finder window; a sidebar, thumbnails of various files and folders appear while a set of icons for managing your files called Toolbar and a search field is at the top of the window.

> ➢ Double click on a file or document to open it. Click once to use shortcuts on the sidebar.
> ➢ Click **View** on the menu bar to change the view of items on display in Finder. You could also use the icons on the Toolbar to have a different view for your files.
> ➢ Press **Command + A** to quickly open the Applications folder. Or click the Applications folder on the sidebar.
> ➢ Click **File > New Finder Window** or press **Command + N** to open a new Finder window.
> ➢ Use a preview pane by clicking **View > Show Preview** or press **Shift + Command + P** use a preview pane. Click **Show More** to see more file metadata. Use the action options at the bottom of the preview pane to perform quick actions.
> ➢ To know the location of a file, turn on the **Path Bar** by clicking **View > Show Path Bar**. This displays the location path at the bottom of the window.

- The status bar is hidden by default. Choose **View > Show Status Bar** on the menu bar to see the size and number of items in a folder.
- Hold the **Command key** and drag apps and items as shortcuts to the **Toolbar**.
- Press **Shift + Command + Full Stop** to show hidden files on your Mac.

The Sidebar

The sidebar is a pane on the left side of the window in Finder. It contains a list of shortcuts to essential folders and frequently accessed locations on Finder for quick access. On the sidebar, you will also find shortcut options to **iCloud Drive** and **Airdrop**.

You can have your favorite items on the sidebar if it is not already there. On the menu bar, click **Finder > Preferences** and select **Sidebar**. Simply drag an item in or out to respectively add or remove it from the sidebar. Press **Option + Command + S** to remove the Sidebar. Use it to also make the sidebar available in Finder.

Searching for Files

Searching for documents is easy. Spotlight can help you track and access files and items on your MacBook Air. Open Spotlight by clicking on the icon in the Dock or selecting it from the menu bar. Also press **Command + Space** to open Spotlight and search for files. Open a Finder window, click on the search field at the top left window to search for files on your Mac. You can access Spotlight in a Finder window using **Command +F.**

As a user, you can change the settings of how you search for files in Finder. When you want to search for files in Finder, the entire system is scanned for the file. But you can limit the search to a folder that is open. Click **Finder > Preferences** and click on the **Advance icon**, then click **Search the Current Folder** in the drop down field.

Chapter 8

Launching an Application on Mac

Launching or opening apps on MacOS is an easy procedure to initiate. Although there are different ways of opening an app on Mac, but still app management is user friendly. If you just swapped Windows for MacOS, you will find out at first that launching an application is different and yet simple. You can launch an app from the Dock, Spotlight, Applications folder, Launchpad etc.

Launch an App Using the Dock

The Dock is one of the first things you will see when you turn on your Mac. It is a row of app icons at the bottom of the screen which is similar to the taskbar on Windows. It is the simplest and fastest way of launching apps on a Mac. It contains essential and commonly used apps which is why the Dock is made available at the bottom of the screen for quick and easy access.

To launch an app, click on the icon of the app in the Dock, the icon bounces and the app opens. A white dot appears below the icon of the app to show that the app is running and active.

You can also have your favorite apps in the Dock for quick access. To add an app to the Dock, drag the app from the Applications folder and move it to the Dock. You may also drag an app out of the Dock to remove it from the Dock; hold the **Control key** and drag it out of the Dock. Removing an app from the Dock does not delete it from your Mac; it can be launched in alternative ways.

When you open an app from anywhere else aside from the Dock, the icon of the app appears in the Dock, but only for as long as the app is running and active. When you close the app, the icon of the app is removed from the Dock. If you want the app to always be in the Dock; hold the **Control key and click on the icon**, select **Options > Keep in Dock**. This way the app will always be found in the Dock.

Launch an App Using Spotlight

If you are new to MacOS, you will find the Spotlight feature really helpful and important. It is a great feature that can do quite a lot on a Mac. It lets you search for anything that can be accessed on your Mac. It is also one of the fastest ways of launching an application. Spotlight is almost accessible from anywhere which is why it is also easier launching apps on Spotlight without quitting what you are doing at the moment.

> ➢ Click on the search icon at the top right corner on the menu bar or press **Command + Space** to quickly open **Spotlight**; a search field appears.
> ➢ Type the name or easily type using initials and Spotlight brings out the top results and other suggested results.
> ➢ Press Return to launch the desired app from the search result. Use the **arrow keys** to navigate search results.

Launch an App Using the App Folder

You can launch an app from Apple's own file manager; Finder. The Finder is basically the center of user operations on macOS. It contains everything from files, documents to pictures, videos, applications etc. In general, Finder is used to organize and browse items and files on MacOS. It can also be used to search for applications and directly launch them. It is usually the first icon on the Dock with the blue and white face.

- Unlike the Program Files on Windows, the Application folder is easy to navigate and use. Open **Finder** from the Dock and click on the **Applications shortcut** on the sidebar pane to look for your desired app.
- On finders, you may also press **Command + A** to open the Applications folder.
- When you see the application you want to launch, double-click on the icon to launch it. Apps downloaded online apart from Mac App Store are found on the Downloads folder. You can also move them to the **Applications folder.**

Launch an App Using Launchpad

Launchpad is the application where you can find all your apps in large icons. When you open Launchpad, an interface that is similar to the interface on iOS devices appears with a search field at the top of the apps and a grid of app icons. Launchpad can be opened from the Dock. It has a gray icon with a rocket ship on it. By default, Launchpad is one of the apps you will find in the Dock when you open your MacBook Air for the first time.

- ➢ Press **F4** to open Launchpad or simply click on the **Launchpad icon** in the Dock.
- ➢ Click an app on Launchpad to launch the app.
- ➢ Apps and programs on macOS may require more than one page on Launchpad, thereby having multiple pages; swipe with three fingers to move across to the other pages. You can click on the dots below the apps to move to other pages and see more apps.
- ➢ You can drag icons around to organize the Launchpad. Drag an icon to the edge of the screen to move it to the next page.
- ➢ Moving an app onto another will create a folder. Rename the folder by clicking on the name of the folder.
- ➢ Quickly search for an app using the search field at the top of the apps and press Return to launch them from the search results.
- ➢ Click on the background and press Escape to close Launchpad.

Closing an App

When you are not using an app, close it by clicking on the red circle at the top right corner of the window, this does closes the window of the app. You can quit an app from the menu bar; Click on the **name of the app** and select **Quit** from the drop down menu. Or press **Command + Q** to quit an app.

Installing an App

The best way to install an app is by installing it from the App Store. Also download them from websites on the internet and install them. Apps can be installed from a disc. Insert the disc and open the disc icon that appears on the screen. In some cases an installer in the disc is used to install the app. It is likely that all you may need to do is to drag the app in the disc to the Applications folder to have the app on your Mac.

Uninstalling an App

Open the Applications folder and look for the app you wish to uninstall. If it has an uninstaller, open it and follow the instructions on screen. Uninstalling an app is different from deleting an app. Use the Trash to remove an app from your Mac and empty the trash.

Spotlight

Spotlight is the search engine on macOS. It does a lot more than searching for items on your Mac. It is a feature that can search for almost anything on a Mac. Spotlight is a feature that you will use very often on a Mac. It is a fast way for looking for items on your Mac and it can be accessed from anywhere on the device.

Spotlight has an index of all the contents in your Mac, which makes it faster for accessing any file. It goes beyond searching for documents and files. It can also perform other operations; it can get you new information from the internet, get directions and locations from maps, do arithmetic calculations, listen to music, find contact details, make unit conversions and a lot more.

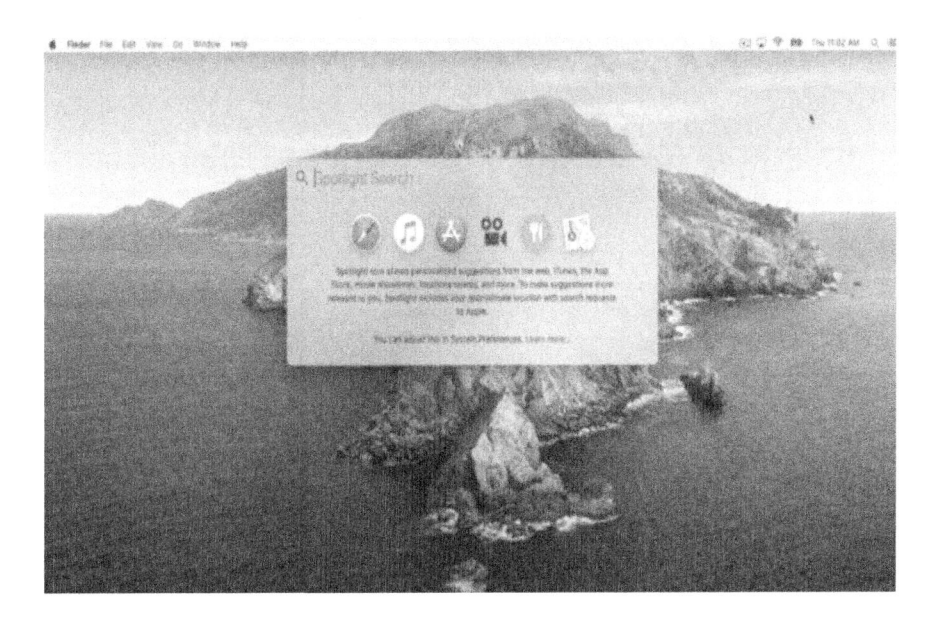

Launching Spotlight

Spotlight is basically used for searching and finding files on your Mac, which is great because it conducts a system-wide search looking for the file. Spotlight can be open with a single click on the menu bar. It is the icon with a magnifying glass – what we all know to be a search icon - on the right side of the menu bar. Click on the icon to open Spotlight from the menu bar. You can use or press **Command + Space** to open Spotlight if you prefer using the Mac keyboard. This is one of the most used and common Mac keyboard shortcuts.

Searching on Spotlight

When you open Spotlight using any of the methods, a search field appears on the screen. This allows you to type in your query. After launching Spotlight, search for the name of the file you wish to open. Spotlight brings out a category of results with the top results – the ones you are most likely to use – at the top.

- Click on a **result** to see more information about the result on the preview pane.
- Navigate Spotlight search results by using the arrow keys to move up and down.

- **Hold the Command key** and use the arrow keys to move between categories on the result list.
- When you find the result you are looking for, select it if it is not already selected on the result list and double click or press **Return** to open it.

Enhance your searching skills on Spotlight using keywords to get the best search results. Keywords such as "videos" will bring out a more specific search result. You can also use phrases, abbreviations and even short forms of the name of apps and files to quickly look for them. If you want to copy a file to a Finder window, simply search for it on Spotlight and drag the result to the Finder window to copy it.

You can modify the categories that appear in your search result and also hide some items from being searched on Spotlight. Go to **Apple menu** and click **System Preferences > Spotlight** to manage or narrow your search results and more.

Chapter 9

Apps on the MacBook Air

Apple has a reputation of making their own applications for their devices. This means that it uses lesser third party applications unlike on other operating systems. The pre-installed apps that come with your Mac make a great ecosystem for operating and performing tasks. The Apple owned apps on macOS are well branded and good enough to perform their respective tasks.

When you open your MacBook Air, one of the first things you will see is the array of applications in the Dock. Some of the apps you will see on the Dock are very useful and core for system operations on the Mac. You can have more apps in the Applications folder in Finder or launch the Launchpad to find more apps on your device.

Apps in the Dock

The Dock is a ribbon at the bottom of the screen. It contains your favorite and frequently used apps. Click on the icon of an app to open it from the Dock. It is better and faster to move an app to the Dock you know you will be in frequent use of the application. Here is a list of important and commonly used apps regularly found in the Dock:

1. **Finder** – This is usually the first app in the Dock. It is the file manager on macOS where you can look at organizing files and documents on the go.

2. **Launchpad** – If you want to use an app that you can't find in the Dock, then open Launchpad and look for the app you wish to use and launch it. Launchpad contains the entire app on your Mac.
3. **Safari** – The default browser on macOS is Safari. Although a lot of people prefer using Google Chrome, Safari takes less power to run. Use Safari to browse and surf smoothly on the internet.
4. **Mail** – Mail is used to manage all your emails and inboxes. It is the default mail app on the Mac Air 2020.
5. **FaceTime** – FaceTime is a popular app on both Macs and iOS devices. It is the video calling application used on Apple devices. However, you can only use the FaceTime app with other Apple devices. You can use other video service apps like Skype on your Mac if you want to communicate with other devices.
6. **Messages** – Send and receive texts using this app. You can use this app with other iMessage Apple devices.
7. **Maps** – You can Maps to get the directions or the location of a place. It is easy to use and navigate.
8. **Photos** – This is where you can view and edit your pictures and videos on your Mac. It is a library that stores pictures and video.
9. **Contacts** – Contacts and contacts details are found in this app. You can sync the contacts on your other Apple devices to your Mac.
10. **Calendar** – Check up on your daily activities on this app. You can manage and view upcoming events.

11. **Reminders** – This is basically a to-do list. Create and make lists of things you want to do on this app. You can also set it up as an alarm.
12. **Notes** – Notes is a great app for jotting down things. You can also use it as a temporary clipboard to copy and paste texts.
13. **Music** – Open Music to see your music library and play a song of your choice. You can also create playlist to put together a list of your favorite songs and also manage the songs on your Mac
14. **Podcast** – Listen to stories and episodes on this app. Subscribe to podcasts and create stations.
15. **TV** – Find movies and shows you like on this application. You can watch television shows and manage them.
16. **News** – News is an icon with a big red N letter that looks more like a division sign on it. You will find it in the Dock on your first time opening the Mac Air 2020. It is a news app where you can get news and headlines from around the world.
17. **Numbers** – Numbers is Apple's very own spreadsheet. Like Excel on Windows, it can do a lot of work on spreadsheets.
18. **Keynote** – On macOS, this is the default app for opening presentations like on Windows PowerPoint. You can view and create presentations and images on this app.
19. **Pages** – Use Pages to type documents and view documents. It is the alternative to Microsoft Word on Windows. It is quite easy and simple to use.

20. **App Store** – The Mac App Store is where you can buy, download and install applications and software. You can also update outdated apps in the App Store.
21. **System Preference** – Aside from clicking on the Apple menu on the menu bar, you can open System Preferences right from the Dock. This, however, is more like a shortcut than an app.
22. **Downloads Folder** – Another shortcut you will find in the Dock at the first time of opening your Mac Air is the Downloads folder. When you download something into your Mac, it is usually downloaded into the Downloads folder unless you change the folder into which you downloaded a file or an item online.
23. **Trash** – At the end of the Dock on the left side is the Trash where you can move files and items you no longer need anymore. Open Trash and click on File on the menu bar and select Empty Trash to permanently remove the file from the drive.

These are all the apps and basically some of the important apps you will need that are in the Dock by default.

Other Apps on the Mac

All the apps on your Mac can be accessed from the Launchpad or from the Applications folder in Finder. Below is a list of other apps you will find on your Mac Air 2020:

1. **Automator** - Automator is an app, which you can use to automate complex and repetitive tasks using workflows on your system. Automator becomes very

useful when you understand how to use it. Beginners can enjoy using Automator.
2. **Books** - This is a library of eBooks, PDFs and EPUBs. You can read, buy and manage books on this app.
3. **Calculator** - You probably can perform mathematical operations on Spotlight. But if it is a problem that looks more advanced, use this inbuilt Calculator on your Mac. It does exactly what a calculator should do.
4. **Chess** - If you love playing chess, then you will be glad to know that your MacBook comes with a chess game.
5. **Dictionary** - Know more about a word from the Dictionary on your Mac. You can also quickly look up the meaning of a word from the Dictionary using Spotlight by searching for the word.
6. **Find My** – "Find My" is a tracking app on your Mac. Use it to find the location of a friend who shares his location with you. You can also use it to keep track of the location of your devices.
7. **Font Book** - This is simply a font management application. You can use it to install, manage and preview fonts on your Mac.
8. **GarageBand** - GarageBand is an inbuilt music studio. It is a useful and nicely equipped audio editing workstation which you can use to make music and create podcasts
9. **Home** - Home is an app which you can use to control smart products in your house. With Home you can control HomeKit devices in your house. You can

control the light bulbs, thermostats etc right from your Mac.
10. **iMovies** - iMovies is an editor for movies and clips. Edit, share and create clips and movies using iMovies.
11. **Image Capture** - Image Capture is used to send images and videos to your Mac. It can also be used with a scanner. It is also used to scan and take pictures.
12. **Photo Booth** - Photo Booth gives you access to the camera on your Mac Air 2020. You can take pictures and record videos on your Mac using Photo Booth.
13. **Preview** - Preview is the default image viewer on macOS. You can view both pictures and PDF files using Preview. It can open different formats of images.
14. **QuickTime** - QuickTime is a media player which can do a lot more on your Mac. It is the default video app on macOS. It can record and play both audio and video, edit them and also make screen recordings.
15. **Stickies** - If you like having sticky notes on your fridge, then you can also have sticky notes in your Mac. Use Stickies to make sticky notes.
16. **Stocks** - Get more information and news around the world about the stock market using Stocks.
17. **TextEdit** - As the name suggests, TextEdit is a text editor. It is for editing texts and is different from a standard word processor.
18. **Voice Memos** - Use Voice Memos to make audio recordings. It can also be used to edit the audios you record.

Utilities on MacBook Air

Utility apps might not be something you will use often. But they can become useful when they are needed. To find utility apps in your Mac, click and open **System Preferences > Applications folder > Utility folder**. Use this keyboard shortcut to access the Utility folder by pressing **Shift + Command + U**. Here you will find all the utilities in your Mac:

1. **Activity Monitor** - Open the Activity Monitor in the utility folder or use Spotlight to search for it and know more about how everything in your Mac is working. See more details about the activities of your storage, processor, application activities etc.
2. **AirPort Utility** - You can manage your AirPort devices on your Mac if you have one. Open the AirPort Utility software and set it up to begin using it.
3. **Audio MISI Setup** - Control the audio devices connected to your Mac. You can manage audio and MIDI devices using this utility.
4. **Bluetooth File Exchange** - Use this to make Bluetooth connections with other devices.
5. **Boot Camp Assistant** - With Boot Camp Assistant you can use and operate a Windows operating system on your Mac.
6. **ColorSync Utility** - Change the color profiles on your Mac system with this tool.

7. **Console** - If you are having issues with your Mac, use Console to do troubleshooting and get diagnostic reports. It opens with logs of messages on the interface.
8. **Digital Color Meter** - This color meter is just like a color picker that gives the color values of a color or pixel on your Mac.
9. **Grapher** - Grapher is used for plotting graphs
10. **Keychain Access** - Keychain Access is the password manager on your Mac. You can retrieve or see a forgotten password using Keychain Access. It stores your login details, account information, Wi-Fi details, generate stronger passwords and it contains a lot more information on your Mac.
11. **Migration Assistant** - This is a great utility for moving your information to your Mac from other devices.
12. **Screenshot** - You can use this tool to take screenshots and make screen recordings on your Mac.
13. **Script Editor** - Use this app to make tools and scripts on your Mac.
14. **System Information** - Find more information about your Mac in System Information. Also use this to get more details about the hardware or software of your Mac.
15. **Terminal** - Terminal is a command line app on macOS. With Terminal, you can gain control of your Mac and oversee a lot more operations unknown to regular Mac users. To use Terminal, you will need to understand how command prompts work to perform a task.

16. **VoiceOver Utility** - This is an inbuilt screen reader. Use this to have the content on your Mac to be read out to you. This feature is great, as it helps people with poor vision to use a Mac.

App Store

Mac App Store is an application storage that contains a huge collection of apps, tools and games, which you can install into your Mac. In the App Store you will find more apps that you can use to do much more on your Mac. If there is a file you want to use or open on and you cannot find it on your system; then visit the App Store. You are sure to find more apps for different purposes right there. Although Mac has provided some pre-installed apps which are useful, some Mac users prefer using a different app which can either be found in the App Store or on the internet.

The Mac App Store is the best and most reliable way to download and install software on a Mac. Apps in the App Store have gone through Apple's inspection to be made available in the store. Apple tries to curb apps that might invade your privacy and increase security risk. This is one of the reasons why some of the apps that you like are not in the App Store. This is also an attempt by Apple to remove malignant software from your Mac.

Downloading or installing an app from the internet is pretty much easy too. But installing apps from the App Store is recommended unless the app is not in the App Store. Although, some apps in the App Store are not free, meaning you would have to purchase them before you can download or install them. Every app you download on Mac App Store will be available to use in the Applications folder or in the Launchpad.

Launching the App Store

The App Store is the blue icon with an A sign on the icon. You can find the App Store icon in the Dock. Click on the icon to quickly open the App Store. You can also launch the App Store from either of the Launchpad, Applications folder or from Spotlight. When the App Store is open, a window appears with apps and stories on the right, while on the left side of the window there is a pane of tabs with a search for at the top of the tabs and a user login at the bottom of the pane.

Before you can install any app on your Mac Air 2020, you will need to sign in with your Apple ID. If you have not done it beforehand, then go to the bottom left corner of the App Store window and click Sign In and sign into your Apple ID account. You will now be able to install apps into your Mac.

On the left side of the App Store is a pane with tabs for quick access. Some of them are:

> ➤ **Search**: The fastest way to look for an app in the App Store is to use the search field. The search field at top of the tabs on the left side of the App Store. Use it to search for apps, tools and games in the Apple Store. Type the name of the app in the search and a list of

results appears. Navigate the list with the arrow keys and press Return to open a result on the list.
- **Categories**: Click Categories to open a list of categories. Some of the app categories are apps for Books, Finance, Music, Kids, Health & Fitness, and Entertainment etc. If you are looking for a particular app based on a topic or for a specific purpose and use, then click Categories and search for the app from the listed categories.
- **Discover**: Discover new apps and tools in the Discover tab. Developers also share their stories and experience to users on how they go about developing these apps.
- **Update**: Use this option for system updates.

Install an App from the App Store

Search for the app using the search field. And open it when it appears on the list of results. Click Get to install the app and wait for it to load. When it is done loading, the Install button appears, click to it to begin installation.

Chapter 10

Touch ID on MacBook Air

The Touch ID is a button positioned along with the function keys at the end on the right side of the keyboard. The Touch ID is a biometric sensor, which can scan your finger and get your fingerprint unless it is wet or foiled with dirt. The Touch ID is an alternative to passwords. But it does not entirely cut out the need for you to enter your password while using your Mac, especially when you need to log in to your account. You will be required to enter your password in some cases.

That being said, with Touch ID you can use it to unlock or wake your laptop when in Sleep mode, switch between multiple accounts, and make purchases with Apple Pay as well as on the various stores in Apple etc.

Setting up Touch ID

Upon booting your MacBook Air for the first time, you will be given the chance to set up Touch ID. Simply place your finger on the Touch ID button and allow it to capture your fingerprint. If you did not set it up at that time or perhaps you want to use multiple fingerprints, you can do just that in System Preferences. Easily set up Touch ID using the following:

> ➢ Click System Preferences on the Dock and select Touch ID. If the icon of System Preferences is not on

the Dock, then select Apple menu on the menu bar and click **System Preferences > Touch ID.**

➤ The Touch ID window appears on screen. Click on the big + sign to register a fingerprint. You will be prompted to put in your password in order to continue.
➤ Place your finger on Touch ID and continuously change the alignment of your finger on the sensor for your fingerprint to be fully captured and registered.
➤ You can check or uncheck the boxes below on the Touch ID window to change the possible applications of Touch ID on your Mac.
➤ You can also have more than one fingerprint but only up to three fingerprints in an account. Across multiple accounts on your Mac, only five fingerprints can be registered.
➤ Hover your cursor about a fingerprint and click on the delete button that appears on the screen in order to remove a fingerprint from your Mac.

Screen Time

Screen Time is a great feature in macOS. It is a feature that gives you or allows you to see information about the time and duration you have spent on each app on your Mac. But apart from just showing and revealing the duration or time we have spent on our Mac, Screen Time can also set a limit on app usage. And if you are a parent, you can also use it to monitor and control the amount of time your child spends on the Mac or any Apple device. With that out of the bag, you can monitor your screen time across your other Apple devices.

Switching on Screen Time:

- Open **System Preferences** in the Dock.
- Click **Options** at the bottom of the pane on the left side of the screen.
- Click **Turn On** at the top on the right corner.
- You can select the **Share Across Devices** box if you want to share the information across all your devices.

You can also set a passcode for Screen Time by marking the **Use Screen Time Passcode** box when you click **Options**. The pane or sidebar on the left shows you the tabs to see app usage on your devices, limit app usage, view all notifications received on your devices and also approve or reject Screen Time requests from your kids.

True Tone

The Retina display on the MacBook Air also works with the True Tone technology in macOS. True Tone is a display sensor which adjusts the appearance and feel of colors on your Mac. The Retina display makes the Mac Air screen resolution great for color. The pixels are packed into a single inch of display, which does not make the colors, and contents of your Mac appear neither vague nor blurry even at a close distance. True Tone makes it just about comfortable for your eyes.

Unless you deal with colors a lot or you are a graphics designer, then you might want to turn off True Tone in order to work or use the proper colors and pixels in your work. The True Tone uses a sense sensor to make the contents display appear automatically natural to you wherever you are using it. To use True Tone:

- Click **Apple menu > System Preferences** or just click the System Preferences icon in the Dock.
- In the System Preferences window, select **Displays**.
- Choose **Display** among the tabs in the window.
- Check the **True Tone box** to make it active on your Mac.

Night Shift

You may also use Night Shift on your Mac. Night Shift allows you to get that warm feel at night when using your Mac Air 2020.

- Open **System Preferences.**
- Choose **Displays** in the window.
- Toggle to the **Night Shift tab**.
- In the Schedule menu box, you may choose to turn it off or set it up automatically from Sunset to Sunrise or use the **Custom option.**
- When you click **Custom**, a timer below the Schedule box appears for you to set an automatic period within which your Night Shift will become active.
- Use the slider below to change the Color Temperature of your Mac to get suitable color warmth for Night Shift.

Chapter 11

Other Mac Features You Should Know

The Magic Keyboard

If you are an Apple fanatic, you most probably are accustomed to using mostly Apple products. While Apple loves to make and improve its own peripheral devices for their products, Apple has since released the Magic Mouse, the Magic Trackpad and the Magic Keyboard. But this year - apparently after so many complaints from Mac users - Apple decided to replace the keyboard on the Mac Air with the Magic keyboard.

Apple replaced the butterfly-mechanized keyboard with the Magic Keyboard and a scissors mechanism. This keyboard is not an external keyboard as widely used with the iPads. Although it does not exactly produce matter from thin air like magic wands in Harry Potter, it has lesser issues that usually hinder the productivity of the butterfly keyboard on a MacBook and it will also give you an excellent typing experience unlike other Macs.

Function Keys

The function keys are shortcut keys, which can be used as controls keys for your Mac. The function keys (F1 to F12) are used to control some of the hardware functions of your Mac such as the volume of the speakers, the brightness of the screen, and some other functions. These control features can be easily identified with the icons inscribed on each button of the function keys:

- **F1** - Reduces the brightness of your screen
- **F2** - Increases the brightness of your screen
- **F3** - Opens Mission Control
- **F4** - Opens Launchpad
- **F5** - Reduces the brightness of your keyboard
- **F6** - Increases the brightness of your keyboard
- **F7** - Skips music backward
- **F8** - Pauses or Plays music
- **F9** - Skips music forward
- **F10** – Mute speakers
- **F11** - Reduces the volume of your speakers
- **F12** - Increases the volume of your speakers

Although, to make use of the standard functions of the function keys, you will have to hold the **Fn key.** The standard functions of the function keys may vary depending on the application in use. So, instead of performing the hardware functions when you hold the **Fn key**, the standard functions of the function keys are actually carried out. You can switch or change this system behavior without always holding or press the **Fn key** to use the standard functions of the function keys; Click System **Preferences > Keyboard** and check the box saying **Use F1, F2**, etc. keys as standard function keys.

AirDrop

AirDrop is a wireless transfer medium that runs on both macOS and iOS. It is a faster way of sending and receiving files from other Apple devices. AirDrop is also available on the Mac Air 2020. You can share pictures, videos and many other things with AirDrop. While using AirDrop, you will be required to turn on your Bluetooth and Wi-Fi for you to possibly share your files and documents with other devices.

Sending and receiving contents through AirDrop

To send a file from your Mac to other AirDrop enabled devices:
- Click on **Finder** in the Dock.
- Select **AirDrop** from the sidebar of Finder.
- You also do this from the menu bar. Click **Finder > Go >AirDrop**.
- AirDrop will prompt you to turn on your Wi-Fi or your Bluetooth if it is not turned on.
- Select the device you want to send the file from the list of nearby devices.
- Then drag the file you wish to send and drop it into the device. And the file is sent to the device.

In some cases, you don't need to directly open Airdrop to send a file to another device or user. You could simply use the Share button:

- Simply open **Finder** from the Dock.
- Look for the file you want to send and select the file.

➤ Click the **Share icon** in the Toolbar of the Finder window.
➤ Select your receiver's device to send the file.

To receive files from other devices, your device should be within range or nearby and discoverable by other devices. If your device does not appear on your sender's device, click Allow me to be discovered by everyone in the AirDrop window. When a file is sent to your Mac with AirDrop a request appears for you to either Accept or Decline the file. Each file you successfully receive is saved in the Downloads folder.

Trash

We get a lot of things into our computer, some of which will no longer be useful in the future. Sometimes, we get items we don't actually need into our computer or a website requires us to download a file in order to continue using the website; disposing these files and items is easy. Files and documents take up space in our computer and when the system storage becomes low; the system begins to lag and does not work quickly. It is frustrating when a laptop takes so much time processing features that should take less time.

Trash is a feature on every computer. On macOS, it can be used to easily remove items from your Mac. On Windows, it is called a Recycle Bin. Trash is something you will most likely use often on your Mac, which is why Trash is in the Dock by default. Obviously, it is the icon with a trash can in the Dock. Click on the icon to open it.

- To delete an item, drag it and move it into the Trash. You may also select more than one file or item, then drag one of the selected items into the Trash and all the items you selected are moved to the Trash.
- Using the menu bar, select the file or multi-select all the files you want to remove and click **File > Move to Trash**. Press **Command + Delete** to also use this feature.
- You may have moved the wrong files to the Trash, which does happen, but recovering files you moved to the Trash is also easy.
- Click on the Trash icon in the Dock to open it. Select the files you want to remove. **Click on File > Put Back** to remove them.
- Also drag the file out of the Trash to remove it from the Trash.

Moving a file to the Trash does not exactly remove it from your Mac. When you move a file to the Trash, the file is not yet deleted from your Mac. Open Trash, click File > Empty Trash to permanently delete all the unwanted items in the Trash or press Shift + Command + Delete to also empty the Trash. When a file or item is deleted from your Mac, it frees up the space it was occupying, thereby increasing the available storage.

Right-Clicking

By now, you already know that you actually cannot right click on your trackpad. If you have previously used a Windows laptop, this will be one of the first few things you will notice on a MacBook. The right click button which is traditionally accustomed to most laptops is omitted from the trackpad design on a MacBook.

The trackpad on the MacBook, however, is usually bigger in size than on a standard Windows laptop. Apple does not have the Right Click button on MacBooks but that functionality is very much available, accessible and also useful in macOS.

Option Click

When you right click an item in your laptop, a pop-up menu appears on the screen with more options for you to choose and use. These options can also be gotten on your Mac Air 2020, hold the Option key and click on the item you wish to get more functions or options from that item. The menu appears with several options for you to use on that item. Some of these options are features or tools you will find on the menu bar or on the Toolbar in Finder.

Trackpad gesture

Holding a key on the keyboard and tapping on the trackpad seems too arduous for a feature you will use quite often. With gestures, you can access this feature right from your trackpad. Tap once on your trackpad with two fingers to bring up the pop-up menu of an item. This is an easier and faster way of using the right click feature on your Mac Air 2020. But if you feel less comfortable with this gesture or holding the Option key and clicking on the trackpad, you can get a third-party mouse with the Right Click button on it.

CONCLUSION: ENJOY YOUR MAC EXPERIENCE!

The Apple Macintosh device is literally one of the astounding computers of the 21st century. As emphasized in this book, the new MacBook Air gives you a stress-free and improvised experience unlike other operating systems. When you favor general quality over raw performance, the 2020 Apple MacBook is your best bet. It has blissful design and an operating system with lots of features to pounce on. All you need do is sit back and enjoy your Mac experience!

About the Author

Konrad Christopher is a video software expert with several years of experience in video-graphy and software development. He is consistent following the latest development in the tech and software industries and has an eye for highend video equipment and software. He loves solving problems and he's enthusiastic about the software market.

Konrad holds a Bachelor's and MSc degree in software engineering from Cornell University, Ithaca. He lives in New York, USA. He is happily married with a kid.

Printed in Great Britain
by Amazon